CAMBRIDGE
UNIVERSITY PRESS

CAMBRIDGE
Primary Science

Workbook 2

Jon Board & Alan Cross

CAMBRIDGE
UNIVERSITY PRESS

University Printing House, Cambridge CB2 8BS, United Kingdom

One Liberty Plaza, 20th Floor, New York, NY 10006, USA

477 Williamstown Road, Port Melbourne, VIC 3207, Australia

314–321, 3rd Floor, Plot 3, Splendor Forum, Jasola District Centre, New Delhi – 110025, India

103 Penang Road, #05–06/07, Visioncrest Commercial, Singapore 238467

Cambridge University Press is part of the University of Cambridge.

It furthers the University's mission by disseminating knowledge in the pursuit of education, learning and research at the highest international levels of excellence.

www.cambridge.org
Information on this title: www.cambridge.org/9781108742757

First published 2014
Second edition 2021

20 19 18 17 16 15 14 13 12 11 10 9 8 7

Printed in India by Multivista Global Pvt Ltd.

A catalogue record for this publication is available from the British Library

ISBN 978-1-108-74275-7 Paperback with Digital Access (1 Year)

Cambridge University Press has no responsibility for the persistence or accuracy of URLs for external or third-party internet websites referred to in this publication, and does not guarantee that any content on such websites is, or will remain, accurate or appropriate. Information regarding prices, travel timetables, and other factual information given in this work is correct at the time of first printing but Cambridge University Press does not guarantee the accuracy of such information thereafter.

The exercises in this Workbook have been written to cover the Biology, Chemistry, Physics, Earth and Space and any appropriate Thinking and Working Scientifically learning objectives from the Cambridge Primary Science curriculum framework (0097). Some Thinking and Working Scientifically learning objectives and the Science in Context learning objectives have not been covered in this Workbook.

Contents

How to use this book

This workbook provides questions for you to practise what you have learned in class. There is a topic to match each topic in your Learner's Book. Each topic contains the following sections:

Focus: these questions help you to master the basics

Focus

1 This plant needs light, water, soil and air.
Draw and label a good habitat around the plant.
Make sure the plant has all it needs.

Practice: these questions help you to become more confident in using what you have learned

Practice

3 Draw arrows to explain each symbol.

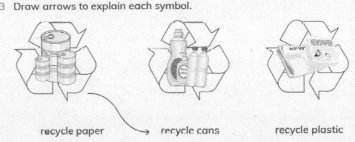

recycle paper   recycle cans   recycle plastic

Challenge: these questions will make you think more deeply

Challenge

3 Finish these sentences.
Use these words.

| move | towards you | stop | away from you |

a A push is a force _____.

b A pull is a force _____.

c Forces can make things _____.

d Forces can make things _____.

4 Write the correct word in each arrow.
Use these words.

| push | pull |

1 ▶ Environments and habitats

> 1.1 Habitats

This local environment is a habitat for many living things.

Focus

1   Draw a living thing from this environment in each of the boxes.

Practice

Look at these two habitats.

One is a cool forest, the other a hot desert.

2   Complete the sentences to say how these habitats are different.

Use these words:

living things   cool   dry   forest   eat   plant

a   A habitat is the natural home of an animal or _____ .

b   The desert habitat is hot and _____ .

c   The forest habitat is _____ .

3   >

d The desert habitat has fewer _____ .

e There are many living things in the _____ .

f The forest animals have many plants to _____ .

Challenge

3 Complete the table.

Say where the bird, tree and rabbit find what they need to live.

Living thing	What each living thing needs	Where they find it
bird	food	on the ground and around the tree
	water	
	home	
tree	light	
	water	
	soil	underground
rabbit	food	
	water	
	home	

> 1.2 Plants in different habitats

Focus

1   This plant needs light, water, soil and air.

Draw and label a good habitat around the plant.

Make sure the plant has all it needs.

2   In the table, draw a circle around the things that the plant will need to grow.

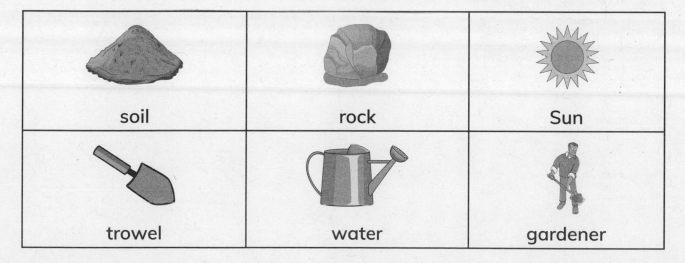

soil	rock	Sun
trowel	water	gardener

Practice

A glasshouse is a house made of glass for plants to grow in.

3 a Draw what you would put inside this glasshouse to make it a good place for plants.

b Label the things you draw.

Challenge

Some habitats are good for plants. Here plants will grow.

Some habitats are not so good for plants. Here plants will not grow well.

Some habitats are so bad for plants that they won't grow at all.

Look at these three habitats.

Marcus plants a seed in each habitat.

4 Complete these sentences to say how the seed will grow.

Use these words:

die   grow   water

a   In the hot desert the seed will _____ .

b   In the cold habitat the seed will _____ .

c   By a river the seed will _____ .

d   The seed by the river grows best because it has _____ .

> 1.3 Animals in different habitats

Focus

1 Look at these animals and these local habitats.

Draw a line to show where each animal might live.

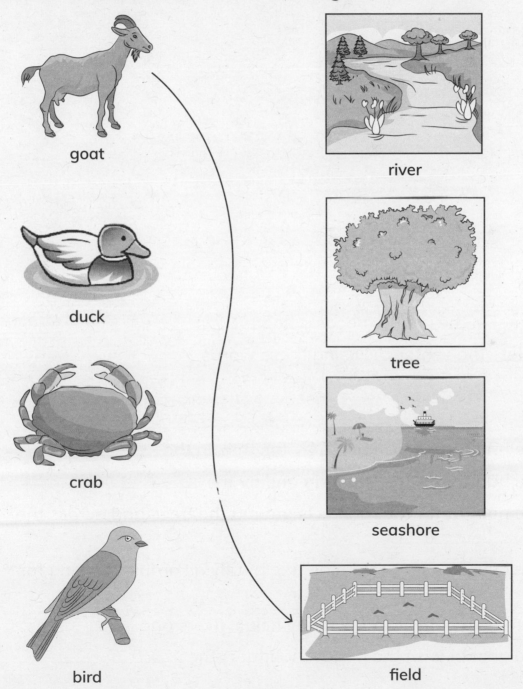

goat

river

duck

tree

crab

seashore

bird

field

Practice

Each animal in the picture needs a habitat.

2 Complete the sentences using these words:

| forests | river | grass | flowers | eagle | fields |

    a The habitat for the mice is by the tree, in the _____ .

    b The habitat for the frog is in and by the _____ .

    c The habitat for the rabbits is around the trees and across the _____ .

    d The bees have a nest in the tree but fly all around looking for _____ .

    e The eagle hunts around many fields, rivers and _____ .

    f The animal with the largest habitat is the _____ .

Challenge

3 Complete the sentences with these words:

plants	habitat	animals	river	grow	die

a Lots of plants live by the _____ .

These plants have a good habitat so they can live and _____ .

b Rabbits and mice eat seeds and _____ .

The snake and eagle eat small _____ .

c A living thing finds what it needs in the right _____ .

Without the things it needs a plant or animal will _____ .

d Now draw arrows on this table to show what plants and animals need.

	light	
	water	
	soil	
plants need →	air	← **animals need**
	food	
	a home	

> 1.4 Rocks and the environment

Focus

1   Draw a line from how we use a rock to the right rock.

How we use the rock	Rock
	**Chalk** A very soft rock used to make sticks for writing.
	**Marble** A hard, strong rock used in floor tiles, wall tiles and to make statues.
	**Coal** A black rock which we can burn to keep us warm.
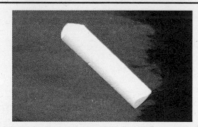	**Slate** Can be blue, purple or grey. It is smooth to touch and often used in floor and roof tiles.
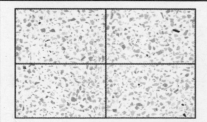	**Granite** A very strong rock used to make bridges and buildings. It has bits in it that are easy to see.

Practice

We dig rocks from the Earth in different ways.

2   Use these words to complete the sentences.

machines   rocks   stones

a   This is a quarry.

On the surface workers use diggers and explosives to

break up the _____ .

Limestone is a rock we dig up in quarries.

b   This is a mine.

Underground workers break the rock with explosives,

tools and _____ .

Coal is a rock we dig up in mines.

c   This is a riverbed where workers dig out sand,

rocks and _____ .

Sand, rocks and stones are used for building.

Challenge

The machine is going to clear the land for a quarry.

3 Finish each sentence to say what will happen.

Use these words:

| home | lost | again | polluted | die |

a The habitat of plants and animals will be _____.

b The river will be _____.

c Many animals may have to move to look for a new _____.

d Very few animals and plants will be able to stay, many will _____.

e Animals and plants may never live here _____.

> 1.5 Can we care for our environment?

Focus

Some children looked at this environment and said these things.

1 Tick (✓) the things which are right.

The plants have been hurt by the people.

Cutting down the trees is bad for the environment.

There is nothing we can do.

Litter in the pond has killed the fish.

2 Draw three things that **you** could do to make the environment better.

Practice

3 Draw arrows to explain each symbol.

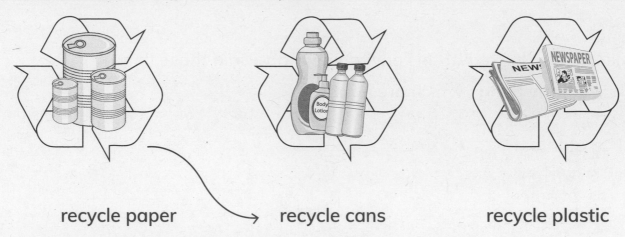

recycle paper　　　　recycle cans　　　　recycle plastic

4 In Dan's class the children recycle paper each day.

Day	Monday	Tuesday	Wednesday	Thursday	Friday
Lessons	English Maths History Technology	English Maths Science	English Maths PE	English Maths Science	English Maths Swimming
Paper pages recycled	70	80	40	70	30

a On which day did they recycle most pages? _____

b On which day did they recycle fewest pages? _____

c Why did they recycle fewer pages on Wednesday and Friday?

_____

d How could the class use less paper?

_____

Challenge

The forest is being cut down to make paper.

5   Sia and Jaz are counting the animals that live in the forest.

Month	January	February	March	April	May	June
Number of animals	65	59	48	42	33	28

a What is happening to the number of animals in the forest?

_____

b If they count the animals in July, what might be the number?

_____

c Where have the animals gone?

_____

_____

d Why have the animals gone?

_____

_____

e How could we protect the animals?

_____

_____

_____

2 ▸ Forces

⟩ 2.1 Forces around us

Focus

1 Draw these things or write their names in the right boxes.

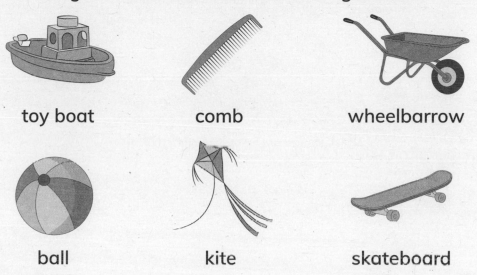

toy boat   comb   wheelbarrow

ball   kite   skateboard

Things I push

Things I pull

Practice

2 Finish these sentences.

Use these words.

| big force | small force |

a

The elephant is using a _____.

b

The ant can push a leaf with a _____.

c

I can move scissors with a _____.

d

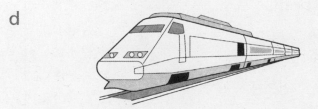

The train needs a _____ to make it move.

Challenge

3 Finish these sentences.

Use these words.

| move | towards you | stop | away from you |

a A push is a force _____.

b A pull is a force _____.

c Forces can make things _____.

d Forces can make things _____.

4 Write the correct word in each arrow.

Use these words.

| push | pull |

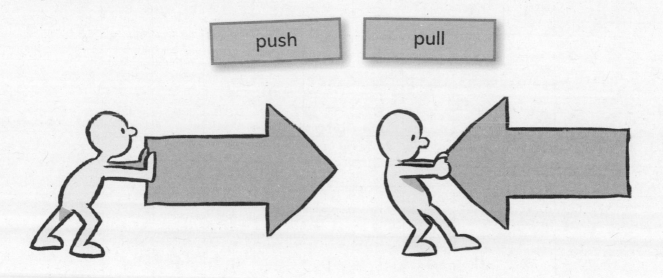

> 2.2 Changing shape

Focus

1 a Find these words in the wordsearch grid.

b Write each word when you find it.

object   shape   change

_____   _____   _____

pattern   height   measure

_____   _____   _____

a	m	e	a	s	u	r	e	t
s	f	u	b	a	z	h	p	w
o	i	p	a	t	t	e	r	n
b	a	i	q	e	p	i	e	b
j	b	c	h	a	n	g	e	x
e	d	l	k	j	g	h	f	d
c	s	a	p	o	i	t	u	y
t	z	d	a	q	f	w	r	t
u	b	a	s	h	a	p	e	e

Practice

Mina is using forces to change the shape of clay.

She is pushing down and rolling the clay.

She counts how many times she rolls the clay.

2 a Measure her piece of clay using paperclips.

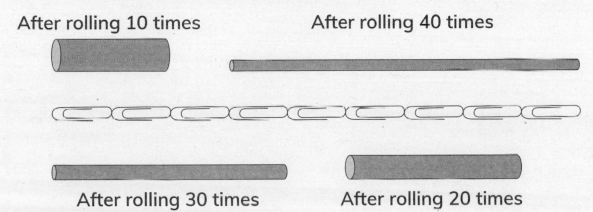

After rolling 10 times

After rolling 40 times

After rolling 30 times

After rolling 20 times

b Write your measurements in the table.

Number of rolls	Number of paperclips long
10	
20	
30	
40	

23 >

Challenge

3 Max also rolls and measures clay.

Here are his results.

Number of rolls	Number of paperclips long
5	2
10	4
15	7
20	10

a How long was the clay after 15 rolls? _____

b How long was the clay after 5 rolls? _____

c How much longer was the clay after 15 rolls than after 5 rolls?

_____

d Choose the right words to finish this sentence.

...shorter it gets.   ...harder it gets.   ...longer it gets.

The more you roll the clay, the _____

e Max's clay got longer than Mina's clay.

Why do you think they were different?

_____

_____

> 2.3 Changing speed

Focus

1   Will these things move fast or slow?

Draw a ring round the correct answer in the table.

Big push →	Small push →	Small push →	Big push →
fast slow	fast slow	fast slow	fast slow

Practice

2   Finish the sentences about this bicycle.

Use these words.

push	speed up

slow down	pull

brake

pedal

_____ the brakes to _____

_____ the pedals to _____

Challenge

3 Sofia is playing on a roundabout.

a How can Sofia go faster?

_____

_____

_____

_____

b How can Sofia slow down? _____

_____

_____

_____

> 2.4 Changing direction

Focus

1 Use these words to finish the sentences.

faster	turn	slower	direction

a A bigger push will make an object move _____.

b A smaller push will make an object move _____.

c Forces can make moving objects change _____.

d Pushes and pulls can make moving objects _____.

Practice

2 How can you get the ball in the net?

Draw an arrow each time to show which way to kick the moving ball.

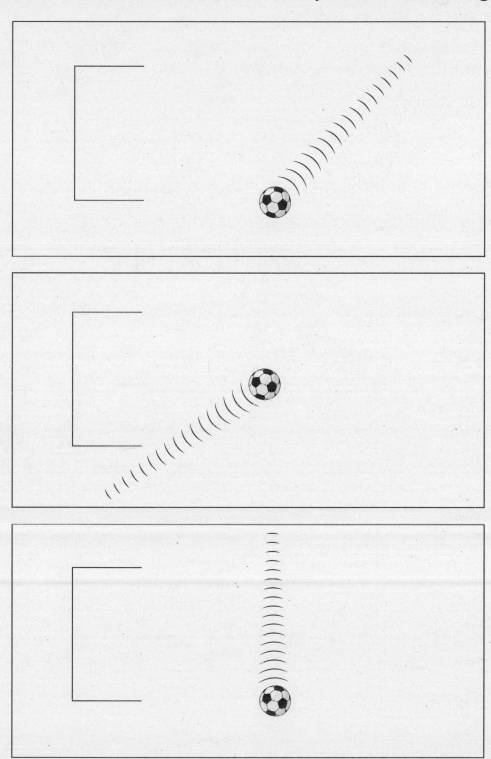

Challenge

You will need: a sheet of paper

Will the paper fall fast or slowly?

3 Predict what will happen each time the paper is dropped.
Write your prediction in the table.

Use these words.

falls fast

falls slowly

4 Drop the paper in different ways. Write what happened in the table.

5 Were your predictions correct or not? Write this in the table.

	A	B	C
What do you predict will happen?			
What happened?			
Was your prediction correct?			

6 Finish these sentences.

A and B change _____.

C does not _____ until it hits the floor.

3 ▶ Getting materials right

> 3.1 Natural and made materials

Focus

1 Are these objects made from natural materials?
   Are they made from materials that have been made by people?

   Draw lines to show if the materials are natural or made.

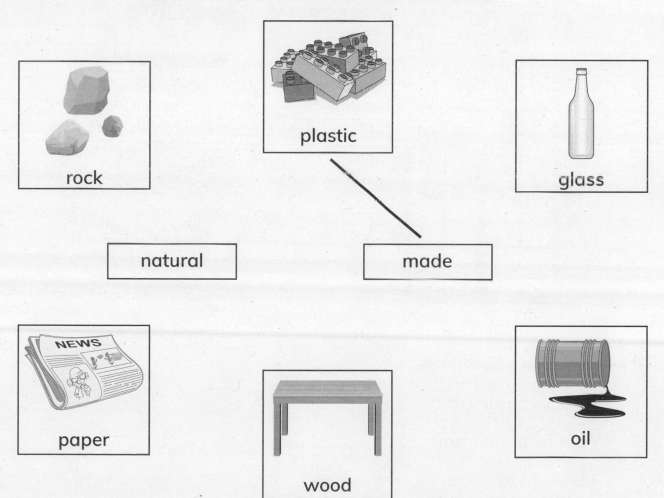

Practice

2 Match these made materials to the natural materials they are made from.

Made materials   **Natural materials**

plastic

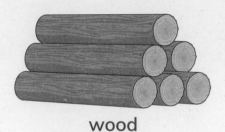

wood

paper

oil

glass

sand

3 Now finish the sentences.

a Plastic is made from _____.

b Paper is made from _____.

c Glass is made from _____.

Challenge

Read this information about wool.

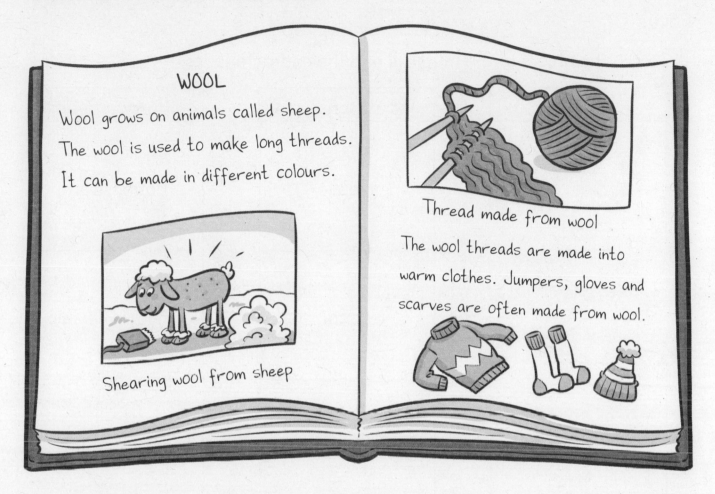

WOOL

Wool grows on animals called sheep.
The wool is used to make long threads.
It can be made in different colours.

Shearing wool from sheep

Thread made from wool

The wool threads are made into warm clothes. Jumpers, gloves and scarves are often made from wool.

4 a Where does wool come from? _____

   b What is wool used for? _____

   c Is wool a natural or a made material?

   _____

⟩ 3.2 Properties of materials

Focus

1 Match the object to the material and the characteristics.

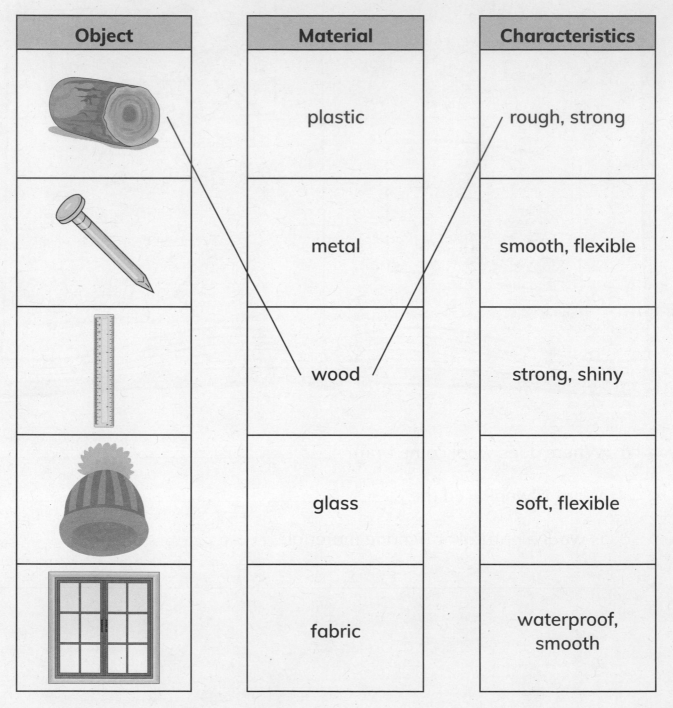

Object	Material	Characteristics
	plastic	rough, strong
	metal	smooth, flexible
	wood	strong, shiny
	glass	soft, flexible
	fabric	waterproof, smooth

Practice

2 Sort these materials using the Venn diagram.

Write the name of the material in the right place on the Venn diagram.

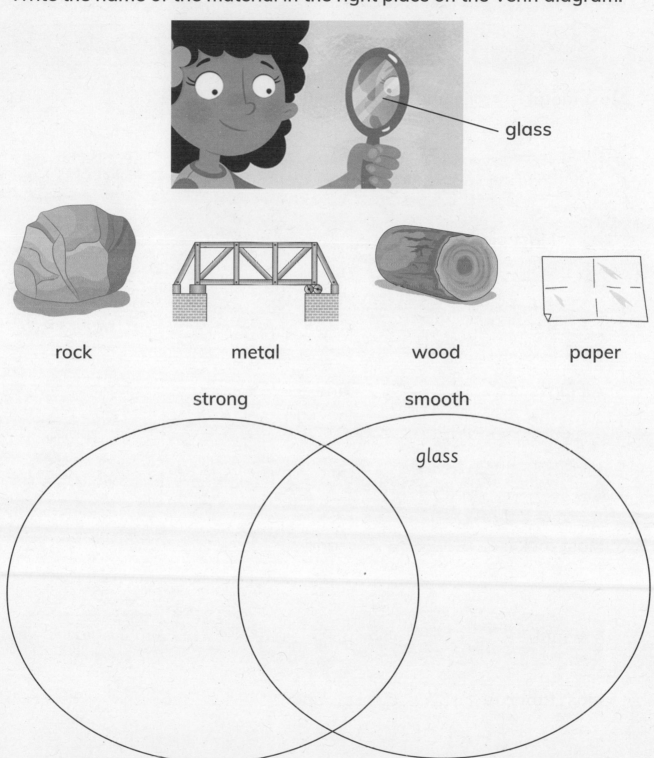

rock   metal   wood   paper

strong   smooth

glass

Challenge

3 Use the right words to finish the sentences.

Example:

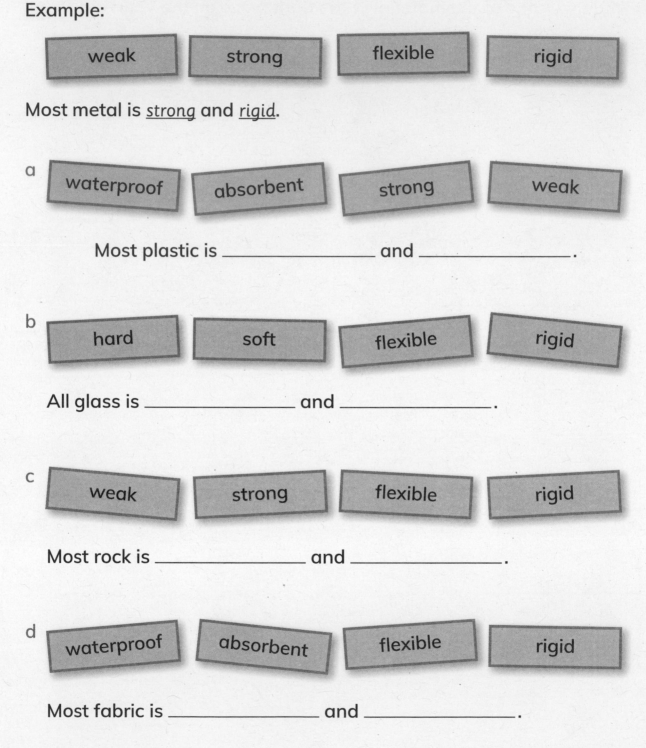

| weak | strong | flexible | rigid |

Most metal is <u>strong</u> and <u>rigid</u>.

a | waterproof | absorbent | strong | weak |

Most plastic is _____ and _____.

b | hard | soft | flexible | rigid |

All glass is _____ and _____.

c | weak | strong | flexible | rigid |

Most rock is _____ and _____.

d | waterproof | absorbent | flexible | rigid |

Most fabric is _____ and _____.

> 3.3 Using the right material

Focus

1   Match each object to the best material and its useful property.

Object	Material	Useful property
	glass	flexible
	rubber	transparent
	metal	absorbent
	fabric	soft
	paper	rigid

Practice

2 Use the right words to finish the sentences.

Example:

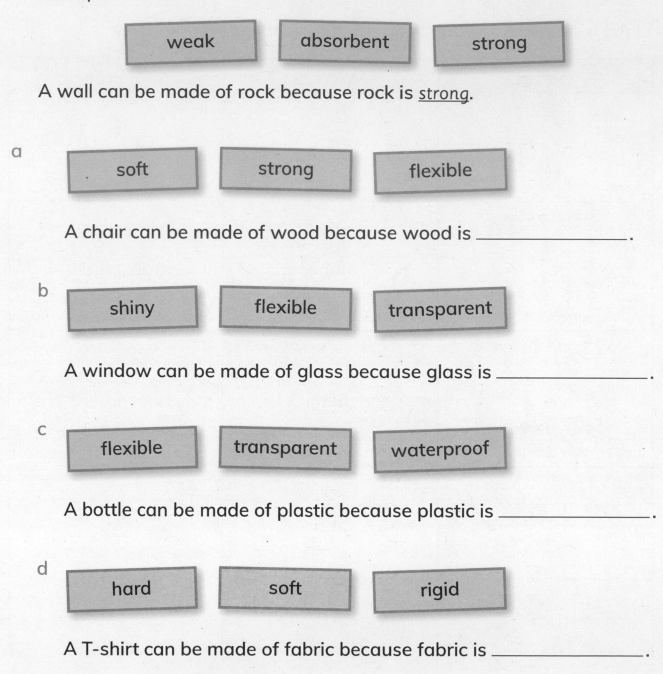

| weak | absorbent | strong |

A wall can be made of rock because rock is <u>strong</u>.

a

| soft | strong | flexible |

A chair can be made of wood because wood is _____.

b

| shiny | flexible | transparent |

A window can be made of glass because glass is _____.

c

| flexible | transparent | waterproof |

A bottle can be made of plastic because plastic is _____.

d

| hard | soft | rigid |

A T-shirt can be made of fabric because fabric is _____.

Challenge

3   Why are these materials used to make a car?

a   The windows are glass because glass is _____.

b   The seats are fabric because fabric is _____.

c   The body is metal because metal is _____.

d   The tyres are rubber because rubber is _____..

> 3.4 Testing materials

Focus

Ben is testing different rulers.

He wants to find out which ruler is the most flexible.

Ben uses bricks to measure how much each ruler bends.

These are his results.

	Wooden ruler	Thin plastic ruler	Thick plastic ruler	Metal ruler
Bricks	2	7	5	3

1 Draw a block graph of Ben's results.

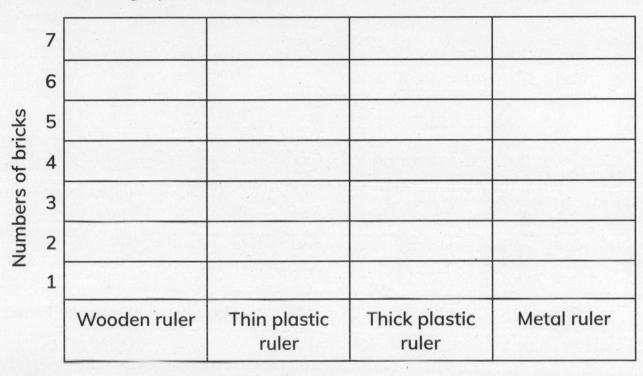

Practice

2 Look at Ben's results in the Focus exercise.

a Which ruler was the most flexible? _____

b Which ruler was the most rigid? _____

c Which ruler was the least rigid? _____

Ben says 'The metal ruler is the least flexible.'

d Is Ben correct? _____

e Why?_____

Challenge

3 Look at Ben's results in the Focus exercise.

a How many more bricks did Ben need for the thin plastic ruler than for the wooden ruler?

_____

b How many more bricks did Ben need for the thin plastic ruler than for the thick plastic ruler?

_____

c Two of the rulers were plastic.
Why did they not bend by the same amount?

_____

_____

d Name a material that would be a silly material to use to make a ruler.

_____

e What properties make this material silly for a ruler?

_____

_____

> 3.5 Changing materials

Focus

1 Draw around the five materials that are changing in this picture.

Practice

2 Write solid or liquid next to these materials.

a _____

b _____

c _____

d _____

e _____

Challenge

3 Add the missing words to these sentences.

melt	solid
solid	liquid

A bar of chocolate is a _____. If you make a bar of

chocolate hot it will _____. This makes the chocolate into

a _____. If you let the chocolate get cold again it will turn

back into a _____.

4 Add the missing words to these sentences.

heated	mixture	different

Butter, sugar and eggs are used to make

a cake. These three _____

materials are made into a _____.

They are then _____ in an oven

to make the cake.

4 ▸ Humans and animals grow

> 4.1 Comparing animals

Focus

What animals can I see in the park?

Zara has a question about animals.

She has done an investigation to find the answer.

Here are her results shown as a tally chart.

animal	bird	spider	cat	ant
Tally	III	I	i	IIII

1 Fill in the block graph.

Numbers of animals				
5				
4				
3				
2				
1				
	bird	spider	cat	ant

Practice

Look at these animals.

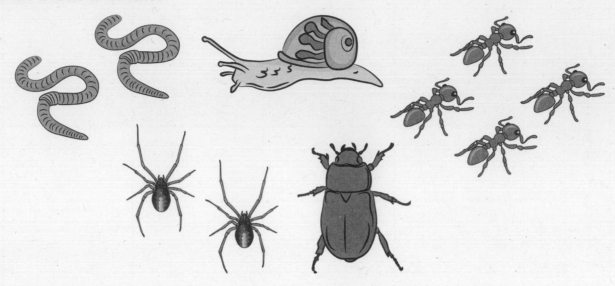

2 Fill in this tally chart.

0 legs	2 legs	4 legs	6 legs	8 legs

3 Fill in this block graph.

Numbers of animals					
5					
4					
3					
2					
1					
	0 legs	2 legs	4 legs	6 legs	8 legs

Challenge

Arun makes a block graph about the colour of animals he found in the park.

Numbers of animals		Black animals	Brown animals	Grey animals
	5			
	4		▓	
	3		▓	▓
	2	▓	▓	▓
	1	▓	▓	▓

4 a How many black animals did he find? _____

   b How many brown animals did he find? _____

   c How many animals did he find altogether? _____

   d How many more brown animals did he find than grey animals?

   _____

> 4.2 Growing

Focus

1   How will this baby monkey change as it grows?
    Put a tick ✓ or a cross ✗ for each sentence.

a   The baby monkey will grow taller.

b   The baby monkey will grow more arms.

c   The baby monkey will grow longer fur.

d   The baby monkey will grow feathers.

e   The baby monkey will grow a longer tail.

Practice

antlers

2 Do these things change or stay the same as the baby deer grows?

Write these words in the correct places.

| changes | stays the same |

a Has antlers _____.

b Number of legs _____.

c Height _____.

d Has a tail _____.

e Pattern on fur _____.

Challenge

Sam has a pet cat. He used bricks to measure how the cat grows.

You can see the results in the block graph.

Numbers of bricks tall	6						
	5					▓	▓
	4				▓	▓	▓
	3				▓	▓	▓
	2		▓		▓	▓	▓
	1	▓	▓		▓	▓	▓
		2 months	4 months	6 months	8 months	10 months	12 months

3 a How many bricks tall was the cat after 4 months? _____

b How many bricks tall was the cat after 8 months? _____

c Sam forgot to measure the cat at 6 months.

Look at the pattern in the results.

How many bricks tall do you think the cat was at 6 months?

_____

d Why does the cat stop growing bigger after 10 months?

_____

_____

> 4.3 Inheriting characteristics

Focus

1 Finish writing each word.

| characteristic | inherit | fingerprint | identical |

a i_____

b i_____

c f_____

d c_____

Practice

2 Chen has inherited her round face from her Dad.

Finish these sentences.

Use these words.

| Mum | Dad |

a Chen has inherited her hair from her _____.

b Chen has inherited her nose from her _____.

c Chen has inherited her ears from her _____.

    d Wei has inherited his hair from his _____.

    e Wei has inherited his nose from his _____.

    f Wei has inherited his ears from his _____.

Challenge

These are the three types of fingerprints.

loop   whorl   arch

3 Look at the fingerprints of these children.

Write their names in the correct place in the table.

Sofia	Arun	Zara	Marcus	Leah

Fingerprint	Loop	Whorl	Arch
Names			

> 4.4 Keeping healthy

Focus

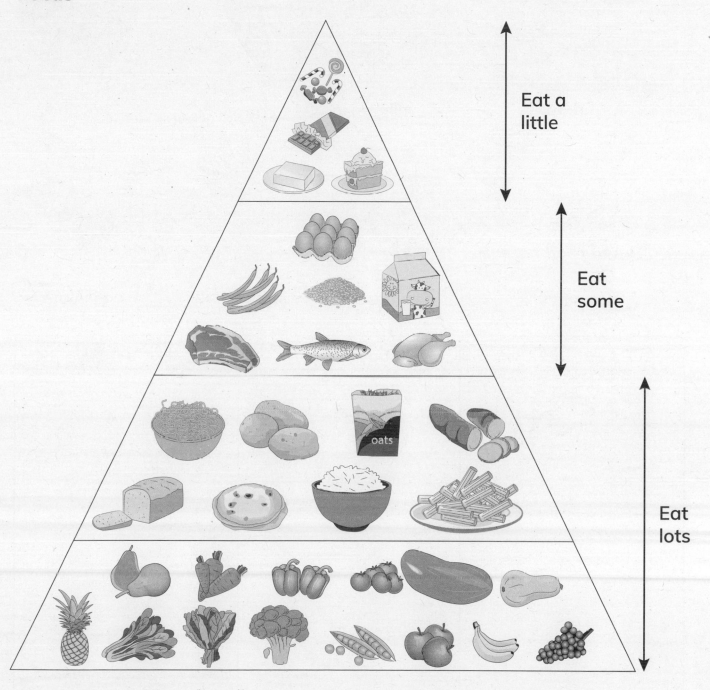

Eat a little

Eat some

Eat lots

This food triangle shows how much or how little of each type of food we should eat.

1 Draw and label these foods in the right group in the table.
The first one has been done for you.

bread   milk   carrot   noodles

cheese   meat   pineapple   chocolate

Eat lots	Eat some	Eat a little
bread		

Practice

2   Use the food triangle in the Focus exercise to plan a healthy meal.
Draw and label your healthy meal here.

Challenge

3 Write the answers in this crossword.

a Do this with water and soap to keep healthy.

b Your skin does this when it gets hot.

c These are things that can make you sick.

d Do this every day to keep your heart and other muscles healthy.

e If you have one of these, you could feel sick.

f This word means the food a person eats.

> 4.5 Teeth

Focus

1   Draw lines to match each tooth to its picture and what it does.

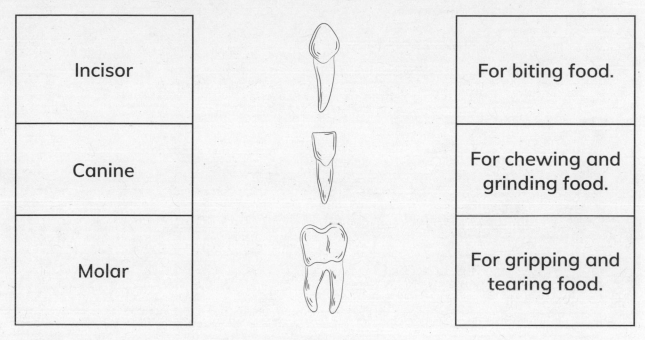

Incisor		For biting food.
Canine		For chewing and grinding food.
Molar		For gripping and tearing food.

Practice

2   Finish these sentences. Use these words.

| toothpaste | dentist | sugar | calcium | fluoride |

How to look after your teeth

a   Only eat a little food that has lots of _____.

b   Make your teeth strong by eating food that has _____.

c   Brush your teeth twice a day with _____.

d   Use toothpaste with _____.

e   Go to the _____.

Challenge

An X-ray is a special photograph that can show our bones and teeth.

3 Label the three teeth with arrows in this x-ray.

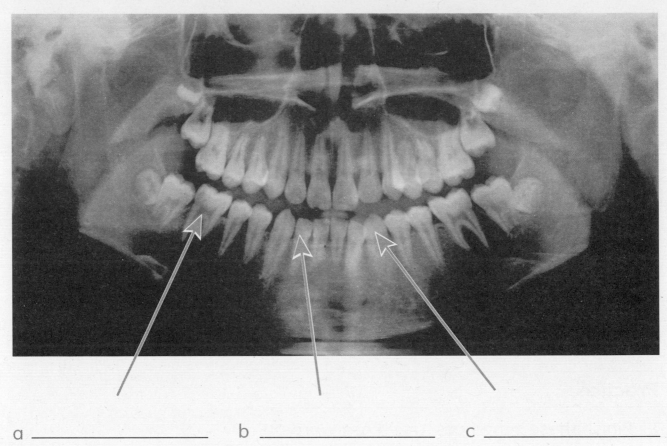

a _____ b _____ c _____

4 The X-ray shows part of the tooth that usually cannot be seen.

What is this part called? _____

5 ▶ Light

› 5.1 Light sources

Focus

1 Look at the picture. Draw (circles) around the light sources.

2 Label the light sources using these words.

| flame | lamp | street light | flashlight |

3 Draw another light source from the picture here.

Practice

4 Look at the pictures below.
Use a ✓ or ✗ to say which is a light source and which is not.

	Is it a light source? ✓ or ✗		Is it a light source? ✓ or ✗

Challenge

The Sun is a light source.

The Moon is bright – it must be a light source.

The Moon is not a light source – its reflects light from the Sun.

Sofia Arun Zara

5 The children can see that the Sun has nearly gone and the Moon is in the sky.

   a Which two children are right? _____

   b Which child is wrong? _____

6 Now use these words to complete these sentences.

| makes its own light | does not make its own light |

   a Sofia is right because she knows that the Sun _____

   _____

   b Arun is wrong because the Moon _____

   _____

> 5.2 Darkness

Focus

Ashrif makes a tent in his classroom.
He has some objects in the tent.

Some are dark in colour.
They may be hard to find.

It looks dark in there.

1   Which objects will be easy or hard to find
    in the dark? Use a ✓ or ✗.

	easy	hard

Practice

Jan is doing science.
She is looking in the box with no light, a little light and lots of light.

2   Choose the right sentence for each picture.

It is light, she can see well.

There is some light, but it is hard to see.

It is too dark to see.

no light _____

a little light _____

lots of light _____

Challenge

Jalil works at night.

head lamp

reflective jacket

computer

3 Answer these questions.

a Why does Jalil wear a head lamp?

_____

b Why does she wear a jacket that reflects light?

_____

c Why is the computer easy to read at night?

_____

d The car driver can see her. Why?

_____

e What could she carry to make her even safer?

_____

> 5.3 The Sun appears to move!

Focus

Look at the picture below.

1. Draw in the Sun at midday.

Practice

Look at the picture below.

2 Draw the Sun's position at three times during the day.

10 am, noon, 4 pm

Challenge

Look at the picture below.

3   Draw an arrow to show the path of the Sun from early morning to late at night.

6 ▸ Electricity

› 6.1 Where do we use electricity?

Focus

Electricity is very useful. Electricity makes lots of things work.

1 Look at the pictures. Do these things use electricity?
   Fill in the table below with a ✓ or ✗.

hair dryer   television   laptop   plant   mobile phone   radio   flashlight

object	Does it use electricity?	
	yes	**no**
hair dryer	✓	

2 Draw two more things that use electricity.

Practice

Some electrical appliances use mains electricity, some use cells.
Some can work on cells or mains.

3 a Do these electrical appliances use cells or mains?

kettle   toy car   fan   mobile phone   laptop   flashlight

  b Draw and write the name of each appliance in the Venn diagram.

Uses cells   Uses mains

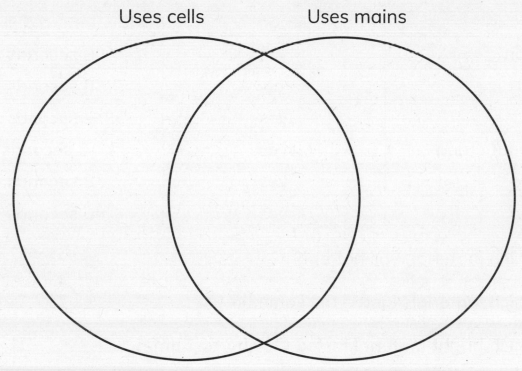

4 Finish these sentences.

  a A flashlight uses cells because _____.

  b A hair dryer uses mains electricity because _____

_____.

Challenge

We use electric lights in our schools and homes.
The electric light bulb was invented by Thomas Edison.

Edison tried 1600 different materials inside the electric
light bulb to make it work.

Some materials were bright and others were not.
Some materials lasted longer than others.
We now use metal inside a light bulb because it
lasts a long time.

5   Look at the table and answer the questions.

Material	Bright?	How long did it last?
Cotton	yes	8 seconds
Wool	no	0 seconds
Hair	yes	2 seconds
Coconut string	yes	12 seconds
Wood	yes	8 seconds
Paper	yes	6 seconds

a   Which material was not bright? _____

b   Which materials lasted the same time? _____

c   Which bright material lasted the shortest time? _____

d   What was the best material? _____

e   Why are electric lights so good to use? _____

_____

> 6.2 Keep safe with electricity

Focus

1 Draw a ⟨circle⟩ around all the dangerous things you can see in the picture.

2 Complete these sentences using these words.

wires	electricity	you

a Keep water away from _____.

b Do not touch damaged _____.

c Never play with electricity, it can kill _____.

Practice

We all need to take care around electricity and electrical appliances.

3   Look at these pictures and explain the danger.

Picture	The danger is

4   Write two rules about electricity. These words may help.

| water | wall socket | damaged wire |

Rule 1: _____

_____

Rule 2: _____

_____

Challenge

Electricity is safe if you follow the rules.

These children are talking about electrical appliances.
These children are wrong.

Water is not always dangerous near mains appliances.

Arun

This radio still works, it must be safe.

Children can touch mains wall sockets.

Sofia

Marcus

Zara

5   Read what they say and then answer the questions.

a   Why should children never touch a mains wall socket? _____

_____

b   Why should you never use a broken mains appliance? _____

_____

c   Zara knows how to be safe with electricity. Write in her empty bubble
    to say what she has to say about electrical safety.

6   Finish the safety poster. These sentences will help.

You could get an
electric shock.

People could trip.

It could start a fire.

They could get an
electric shock.

> 6.3 Making circuits

Focus

1 Look at these electrical things. They are all used in electrical circuits.
  Say what each thing is called and what it does.

Name	Object	What does it do?

2 Draw a complete circuit using the objects shown in the first part of the Focus exercise and two wires.

Practice

3 Look at the pictures.
Under each picture write a sentence to say what will happen.

You can use these words.

The lamp   does   does not   light up

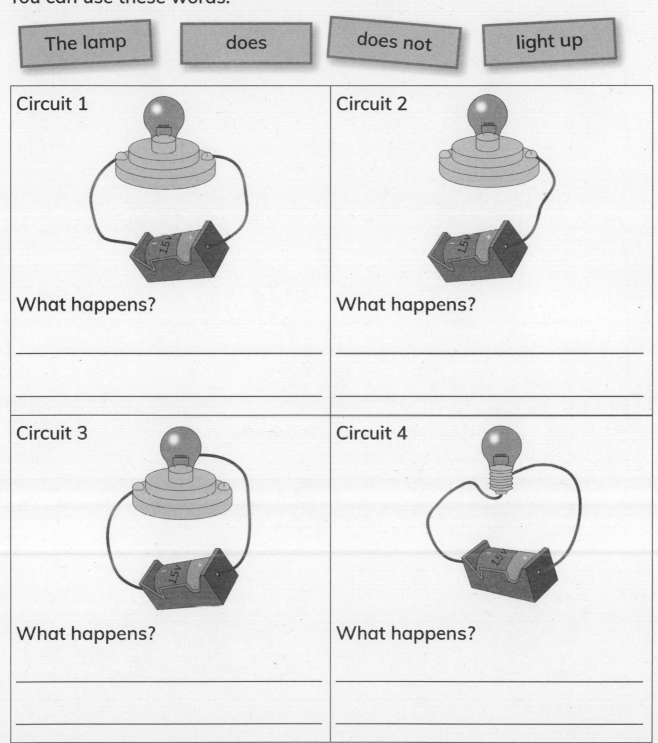

Circuit 1

What happens?

_____

_____

Circuit 2

What happens?

_____

_____

Circuit 3

What happens?

_____

_____

Circuit 4

What happens?

_____

_____

4 Draw another circuit that will not work. Write what is wrong.

Challenge

We can make many different circuits with lamps, cells and wires.

If we use small cells, the circuits will be safe.

5   Look at these circuits and then answer the questions.

   The cells and lamps are all the same.

Circuit A

Circuit B

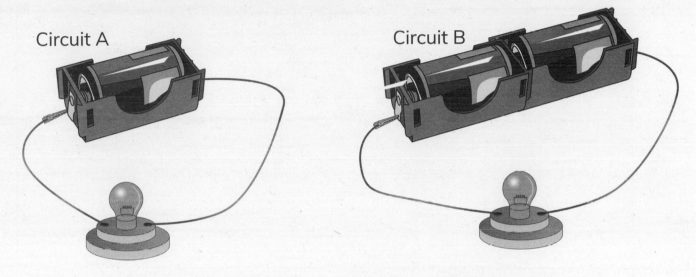

Circuit C

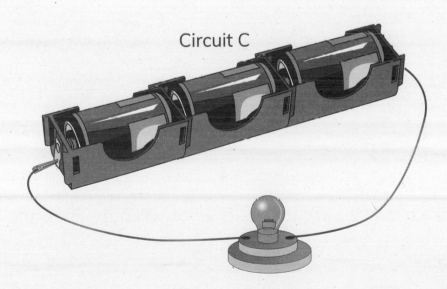

a Draw arrows on each circuit to show the flow of electricity around the circuit.

b Which circuit will have the brightest lamp? _____

c Why is this lamp brightest? _____

d How could we stop circuit C working? Draw this.

e If we make a circuit with four cells what will happen to the lamp?

_____

_____

_____

Acknowledgements

The authors and publishers acknowledge the following sources of copyright material and are grateful for the permissions granted. While every effort has been made, it has not always been possible to identify the sources of all the material used, or to trace all copyright holders. If any omissions are brought to our notice, we will be happy to include the appropriate acknowledgements on reprinting.

Cover by Pablo Gallego (Beehive Illustration)

Thanks to Getty Images for permission to reproduce images:

Inside Unit 1 James O'Neil/GI (x2); Andresr/GI; magnetcreative/GI; Germán Vogel/GI; Vm/GI; Andresr/GI; Deepspace/GI; Mangiwau/GI; Unit 2 Creative Crop/GI; Unit 4 Markus Schneider/GI; Herbert Kratky/GI; FotoFeeling/GI; Tara Reifenheiser/GI; Yagi Studio/GI; Unit 6 SSPL/GI

GI = Getty Images